AF116765

New Life Clarity Publishing
205 West 300 South, Brigham City, Utah 84302
Http://newlifeclarity.com/

The Right of Isabelle Thrapp to be identified as the Author of the work has been asserted by her in accordance with the Copyright Act 1988.

New Life Clarity Publishing
name has been established by NLCP Corp.

All Rights Reserved.
No part of this publication may be reproduced, distributed, or transmitted in any form or by any means, including photocopying, recording, or other electronic or mechanical methods without the prior and express written permission of the author or publisher, except in the case of brief quotations embodied in critical reviews and certain other noncommercial uses permitted by copyright law.

Printed in the United States of America
ISBN-
Copyright@2024 Isabelle Thrapp

Girls are *Amazing*

By
Isabelle Thrapp

About The Author

Isabelle Thrapp is a teenager living in Utah. She is the oldest of three children. She loves learning anything and everything, especially history and language arts. She loves to draw, paint and color. Isabelle enjoys being outdoors, like snowboarding/sledding, bike rides, and boating. She also enjoys hanging out with all her friends. One fun fact about her is she has a very large extended family with over 100 cousins, aunt/uncles, and second cousins. Isabelle has been tumbling/dancing since she was 4, and loves it alot! She hopes to be on the cheer team in high school. In fifth grade, she was awarded the Mayor's Award, for her outstanding public service. Isabelle has always been a big reader and writer, as she read Junie B. Jones in kindergarten and started writing books in first grade. In fourth grade, she even started a neighborhood newspaper with some friends called "Neighborhood News." Isabelle is so excited and happy that she was able to have a book published!

Dedication

To my Mom, She is the whole reason I am doing this. To my dad for encouraging me along the way. To Elizabeth and Jonas for being so excited about this with me! In addition, to my wonderful friend and publisher, for making this happen. Thank you!

Table of Contents

Introduction … xi
Chapter One: Ruby Bridges- The Brave One … 1
Chapter Two: Anne Frank- The Author … 13
Chapter Three: Malala-The Survivor … 25
Chapter Four: Amelia Earhart- The Defier … 33
Chapter Five: Princess Diana- The Giver … 43
Epilogue … 53

Introduction

When I was about eight or nine, I started to notice the differences between girls and boys. Girls were supposedly not as strong. They were supposed to look pretty. However, no one cared how boys looked. We were all supposed to have crushes, and like makeup. The sport that most girls liked was dance.

Now granted, I fit pretty well into that mold. I have crushes, I love makeup. I love tumbling and cheer, and I still like to dance. Nevertheless, what about the girls that did not like those things? They were seen as weird.

In fifth grade, I did a pentathlon. Every fifth grader had to do it. We did high jump, long jump, 40-yard sprint, 40-meter dash, and shot put. It really bothered me that girls and boys were scored separately. I won second place in the high jump. The girl who got first place beat the boys by a long shot. So why couldn't we be scored together? I got tired of hearing "Girls are just built differently than boys." What is that supposed to mean?

My fifth grade teacher was in charge of teaching us to throw the shot put, which is a heavy ball you throw as far as you can. I threw as far as I could, but it did not go very far. "That was pretty good for a girl," he said. I do not think he was trying to be mean, but it made me mad. He probably meant it as a compliment. It made me work extra hard. When we got to choose which spot to spend extra time on, many days I spent it there to prove to him I could be just as good as the boys.

In the end, I did not get any awards for the shot put, but I know I improved a lot. My arms are much stronger today than they were then, but I still do not think that shot put is my thing. That is ok. I just wanted my teacher to know that we girls are strong too!

Around that time, I also noticed that there were not many women that we learned about at school. For that matter, there were not any girls!

Introduction

When Pattie Godfrey~Sadler (my publisher) said that I was receiving the Publishers Sponsorship Scholarship, she told me I needed to think about what is important to me. Almost immediately, I knew I wanted to write about <u>Girls </u>in history.

These girls are my favorite. I know I do not know them personally, but I love them so much! Ruby Bridges showed me that I could be any age and still make the biggest difference. Anne Frank inspired me to keep writing when I thought I should stop. Malala is one of the most amazing people this world has seen. Not only did she fight for her and other girls' rights before she was shot, but after too! She did not let anything stop her, so neither am I. Amelia Earheart proved that you do not have to be girly to be a woman. Princess Diana showed us that everyone is important. She showed us that we need to care for everyone we meet, even if we think we are better than they are (let me give you a hint… you are not better than anyone, and no one is better than you are.) **We are all the same, equal**.

Even though we do not learn about girls at school, I want to make sure that every girl or woman knows about the amazing people that have helped shape our world.

Chapter One:
Ruby Bridges- The Brave One

*"We keep racism alive. We pass it on to our children.
I think that is very sad."*

Ruby Bridges was born on September 8, 1954. She lived in New Orleans. That is a big city where they have one of the biggest Mardi Gras celebrations. Mardi Gras is a fun Carnival like celebration, and New Orleans goes all out. It is to celebrate the harvest. This is celebrated during February, on the Tuesday before Ash Wednesday.

Ruby started to take care of her siblings at a very young age. She had to take care of them because her parents had to work for a lot of the day. She had to feed, and clean her siblings. She had to clean up their messes. She had to make sure they were entertained. Have you ever taken care of your siblings?

When Ruby went to kindergarten, she went to a segregated school. This means that everyone in her school was darker skinned. This does not happen anymore because it is illegal. At this time, it had just become illegal, so not very many people followed the law that said their schools could not have only colored or only white people. This mostly happened in the south.

At the end of kindergarten, all of the kindergarteners at Ruby's school took a test. Those who passed would go to the white school in first grade. However, not very many kids did, because the white people made it extra hard so that less black kids would pass it. The white people did not want black kids in their school. Still, Ruby passed.

In the fall, Ruby's parents were asked if she could go to William Frantz Elementary School. This was the school for white kids. Ruby's father did not want her to go, but eventually her mother convinced him to let her. They told her that she would have to be escorted (or taken) to school by the federal marshals. Imagine a big bodyguard like the ones you see in the movies. Those were the federal marshals. They were in charge of protecting Ruby.

Six children were asked to go to white elementary schools. However, in the end, two of them decided to stay at their old school. Three of them were sent to McDonough No. 19. They were nicknamed the "McDonough three". That only left… Ruby. She was told that she would go to Frantz *all by herself.*

On her first day of school, she thought that it was the Mardi Gras celebration because when she got there, people were screaming, and throwing things, as if they would at a parade. She did not know that it was because of her though.

She and her mother (who came with Ruby on her first day) were told to walk straight into the school, not look at the crowd, and not stop. The four federal marshals would be on each side of her, like a square.

Ruby walked up to the school like a proud little soldier. This little skinny black girl with the curliest hair you ever saw marched right up to that school so bravely. She had long lanky arms and legs that swung with confidence. She held her head up high and proud, her small trusting smile could be seen. She was excited to go to a new school!

Ruby Bridges Walking into School

When Ruby got into the school, she did not go to class. She sat in the principal's office all day. No one else went to school either. All of the students' parents pulled them out as soon as they saw that Ruby had gone into their school.

One of the reasons Ruby sat in the principal's office all day is because they had no one to teach her. Then, Barbra Henry, a teacher from Boston, Massachusetts, said she would work with Ruby. Mrs. Henry was the *only one* that was willing to teach Ruby.

The next day, Ruby came to school, but without her mother. She went into Mrs. Henry's room, but there was nobody else. Where was everyone else?

There were no children at the school at the time. Nobody wanted their children in a class with a little black girl. Therefore, Mrs. Henry taught Ruby as if she was an entire class of first-graders.

After a while, Ruby started to see a child psychiatrist named Robert Coles. A child psychiatrist is a person who helps children to be happier. If they need it, they can prescribe medicine to the children. They also study the way children behave in certain situations to better understand them and help them. Mr. Cole told her to draw pictures, and he started to understand the strains that Ruby was dealing with. She was scared about the people in front of the school. She was anxious all the time. She was nervous that something was wrong with her. She had to be sent to a different school, and then was in a separate class to everyone else. Why was she always scared? Why was she being treated differently? Have *you* ever felt scared or different?

The Problems We All Live With

Meanwhile, the city was targeting Ruby's family. Her father lost his job. Her grandparents' home was burned down. Even the store they went to told them they could not shop there anymore.

Years later, it even caused her parents to be separated. Ruby's family started to realize that this was having a strain overall on the family, not just Ruby.

One time on her way into the school, Ruby stopped on the steps. She turned around. She started to talk. The federal marshals asked her to go into the school, but she would not move. Finally, she walked up the stairs, into the school. When she walked into Mrs. Henry's classroom, Mrs. Henry asked her what she was saying to the crowd. Mrs. Henry was watching the whole time, and she was very scared. Nevertheless, Ruby told her she was not talking to the crowd.

Mrs. Henry was confused. She asked her what she *was* saying. She told her that right before they got to school every day, she would stop and pray. But that day, she had forgotten to. So, when she remembered on the steps, she prayed. She asked God to forgive the people who said mean things about her and threw things at her.

Ruby would always eat lunch by herself in the classroom. After a while, she stopped having an appetite.

Imagine eating lunch by yourself. It would not be very fun, would it? A little girl, all alone. Her small, defined eyes looked hopeful, yet sad.

She could hear the other kids in the cafeteria, and Ruby *really* wanted to join them. She blamed not eating on the fact that her mother always made peanut butter sandwiches. She started to hide her sandwiches in the storage closet, and put her milk in the paste (glue) jar. She thought that not eating lunch would somehow get her to the lunchroom.

Ruby Bridges and Kamala Harris

Eventually, when mice and roaches started to appear, the janitor found Ruby's sandwiches in the closet.

In her book *Through My Eyes*, she said, "Mrs. Henry wasn't mad at me. She was just sorry there were so many days when I hadn't eaten."

After that, Mrs. Henry sat with her at lunch. They laughed and talked, and Ruby felt included again.

For a little while, she had trouble eating at home too. She would only eat potato chips and sodas. She could not remember why she stopped eating. Truthfully, however, there had been a woman who stood outside the school who threatened to poison her to death. This was probably the root cause.

By the end of first grade, she was able to play with other white kids, who started to go to school. The children's parents eventually figured that a little black girl should not stop their kids from getting a good education.

Around that time, the white people who stood outside of the school yelling had decided that they were bored of harassing a little girl. She had a few hours of class time with the other kids, instead of being all by herself.

Unfortunately, Mrs. Henry was not back the next year. Instead, Ruby was put in a regular class with other kids. Ruby Bridges was the one who started the integrating process. Integrating is the process of combining the white kids with the black kids.

Since then, Ruby has fought black equality. She has also helped with women's equality. She has even met with President Barack Obama.

Ruby Bridges Giving a Speech

We need to be more aware of the things that we are introducing or saying to our siblings and friends, and when we are older, to our children.

Ruby Bridges was a brave, strong little girl. How can you be braver like Ruby?

"Kids come into the world with clean hearts, fresh starts."

Visit Ruby at her website: rubybridges.com.

Chapter Two:
Anne Frank- The Author

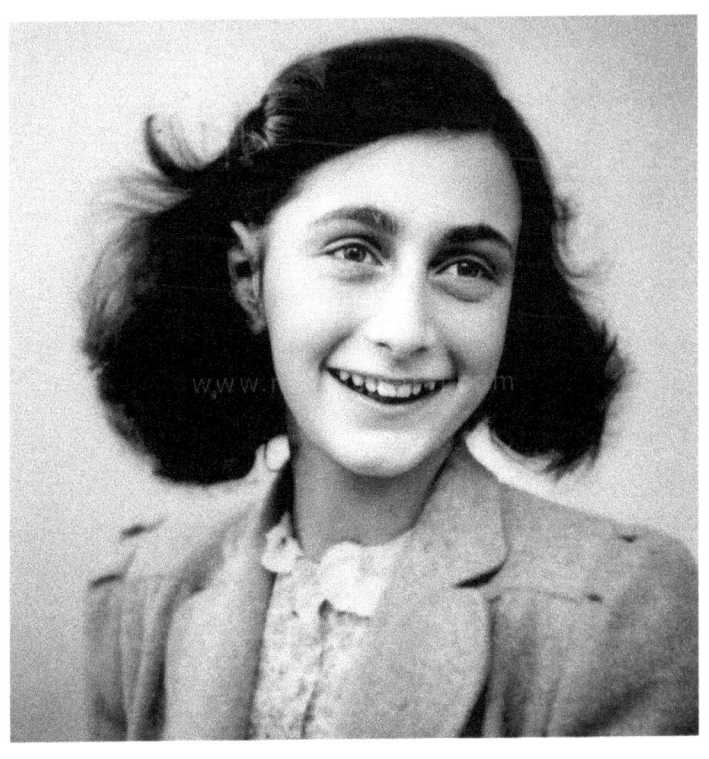

"No one has ever become poor by giving."

Annelies Marie Frank was born on June 12, 1929. She lived in Frankfurt, Germany until she was four. During this time, the beginning of World War 2 began. The Franks' had to move to Amsterdam, Netherlands to avoid the conflict. The Jewish People, like Anne, felt safer in places like the Netherlands than in Germany because that is where the conflict was starting. Have you ever moved?

Ever since Anne was a very young girl, she wished that she could be an author. Have you ever thought about what you want to do when you grow up? Not everyone knows at such a young age. What do you want to be when you grow up? It is ok if you do not know yet. Anne wanted to be published in a newspaper or a magazine. However, she did not think she was good enough to be published. She still loved to write and would write down her thoughts on a regular basis. It is amazing that she just kept at it and so a record was created of her courageous life. She never gave up!

Anne's religion was Judaism. Jewish families celebrate things like Rosh Hannah, Shabbat, Yom Kippur, and many more holidays that are fun. In the Jewish Religion, they believe in the Old Testament and follow the Ten Commandments. Anne was very proud to be a Jew, and she did not hide it.

While her sister Margot was a Star Pupil, Anne was smart, but mischievous. She would often play tricks on her teachers and friends.

In 1941, Anne and Margot were forced to leave their school that they had been going to. They had to go to a special Jewish school, as it had become a law. They were not allowed to go to a regular school.

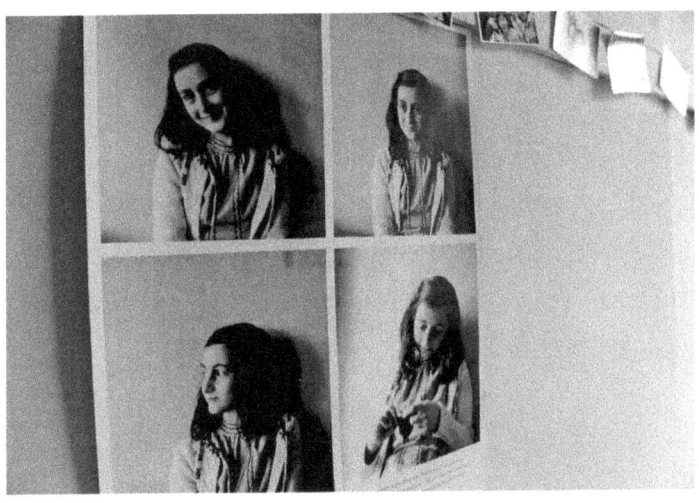

Anne Frank

This was just the start of Jewish regulations. Some others included having to wear a star on their sleeve at all times, (so that they could be identified), many jobs were unavailable to Jews, many stores they could not go into, and many more limitations on their freedom. Many Jews started to feel restricted.

For Anne's thirteenth birthday, her parents gave her a diary. Anne named this diary Kitty, and every time she wrote in it, she would start by saying "Dear Kitty,"

Eventually, the Franks decided that they were going to need to go into hiding. The Germans were abducting Jewish families very often at this point. They prepared for several months. However, 10 days before their leave day, they got a letter saying that Margot needed to be relocated to a labor camp. Labor camps were the way that they started to separate the families from each other. These labor camps were dangerous and deadly. They worked the people to death, not letting them bathe, and giving them almost no food or water. Fearful for their family, they went into hiding early. In order to carry everything that they needed, they had to wear many clothes, although it was July, and very hot and humid. They left their house slightly messy, and a note implying that they were going to Switzerland. Sadly, Anne also had to leave her cat, Moorje, and was heartbroken. She also gave her special marbles to her friend to keep them safe.

The Franks were forced to walk all the way to their new house, because Jew's were not allowed on public transportation. Sneaking through the streets and trying to remain unseen was difficult but they finally arrived at their destination.

Secret Annex bookcase door, Miep, and her husband, Jan

The Franks moved into a hiding place at the back of a company building. They called this place the Secret Annex. In the Secret Annex, the Franks had "Helpers". These "Helpers" brought food, news, and entertainment (like books) to the Frank family. Their helpers were Victor Kugler, Johannes Kleiman, Miep Gies, and Bep Voskuijl. These "Helpers" took a great risk in helping the Franks hide. If caught, the crime of sheltering Jews was punishable by death. Nevertheless, they continued to help Anne's family anyways.

Peter, Hermann and Augutse van Pels, and Fritz Pfeffer later joined Anne's family. Fritz was a dentist. All of them had suffered the same persecution as the Franks. Anne loved having other people to talk to, though in her diary she tells of the many disagreements between the families.

Anne did have her own opinions about each person though. She thought that Mrs. van Pels was selfish and the 'Busy housewife'. She thought that Mr. van Daan (nickname last name Anne gave to the van Pels) was also selfish because of all the food that he and his wife ate in the beginning. Anne also had a certain opinion about Fritz; she thought he was foolish and annoying. Anne had to share a bedroom with Mr. Pfeffer, the dentist.

Anne wrote all things down in her precious diary. One of the most memorable excerpts is this one:

"I finally realized that I must do my schoolwork to keep from being ignorant, to get on in life, to become a journalist, because that's what I want! I know I can write ..., but it remains to be seen whether I really have talent ...And if I do not have the talent to write books or newspaper articles, I can always write for myself. But I want to achieve more than that. I can't imagine living like Mother, Mrs. van Daan and all the women who go about their work and are then forgotten. I need to have something besides a husband and children to devote myself to! ...I want to be useful or bring enjoyment to all people, even those I have never met. I want to go on living even after my death! And that's why I'm so grateful to God for having given me this gift, which I can use to develop myself and to express all that's inside me! When I write I can shake off all my cares. My sorrow disappears, my spirits are revived! But, and that's a big question, will I ever be able to write something great, will I ever become a journalist or a writer?"

During her stay in the Annex, many of her fights were with her Mother. She was a Daddy's girl, and struggled to get along with her mother. Although she loved her mom, it was easier for her to feel safe with her dad. Have you fought with your parents?

Much later into her time in the Secret Annex, Anne started to have a romance with Peter. She even had her first kiss while there. Her short romance with him was special to her.

Anne Frank Wall of Celebrities

Anne tells about her life in her diary, and much of her time is spent reading, writing, or doing schoolwork.

On August 4, 1944, the Nazis police caught Anne, her family, the van Pels family, and Fritz. Anne was sent to a labor camp. She died while there, most likely of Typhus. Anne was only 15 years old.

Only 2 weeks after she died, the war ended. Anne's father, Otto, was the only one to survive the war from the Secret Annex. The others all died at the concentration camps. Miep, who was one of the only surviving "Helpers", found Anne's diary after the war. This consisted not only of her red and white book, but also of separate leaflets or pieces of paper.

Miep gave Anne's diary to Otto. He did not want to read it at first, because he felt like he was invading her privacy. Eventually, he read it, and realized what an accurate description of their life she had recorded. He said some parts were painful to read because he missed Anne, and their family, and he remembered all the things she talks about in her diary.

Anne Frank

Otto decided that he should fulfill Anne's dream of becoming an author. He pitched a publisher and was rejected. Although he was turned down, he was not discouraged. He would not let his daughter's dreams go. He tried again, and a publisher accepted his work. Since the publishing in June of 1947, there have been 30 million copies sold.

How can you start working toward your dreams? How can you record your life?

"I must uphold my ideals, for perhaps the time will come when I shall be able to carry them out."

Visit her at her website at https://www.anne-frank.org/en/anne-frank/.

Chapter Three:
Malala-The Survivor

*"One child, one teacher, one book, one pen
can change the world."*

Malala Yousafzai was born on July 12, 1997. Her name means grief-stricken, though she is full of joy. She is an impressive Muslim girl, known for fighting for human rights, mainly women's right to education. Like Anne Frank, Malala's religion is an important part of her life. Muslims believe in one god. Their scriptures are the Torah, the Psalms, the Gospels, and the Quran. Malala read these often. She also prayed often. Another part of her religion is that they all have to wear burkas when they come of age. Have you heard of a burka?

At age 11, Malala wrote a blog for the BBC Urdu. For safety reasons, she wrote under the pen name Gul Makai, which means CornFlower. That way, they could not track her down, as her real name was not revealed. She wrote about what life was like under the Taliban rule. She was teaching the outside world about the things that were happening in her country, because most people did not know about it. She often wrote about her family's fight for girls' education rights. She told of how she and her family were fighting for girls to be able to go to school in their community. Her blog ended on March 12, 2009. She was also in a documentary for *The New York Times* in 2009, before she became famous.

Young Malala

The Taliban (the ruling party) decided that they were going to ban TV, music, girl's education, women from going shopping and more. After this ban, only 11 out of 27 girls continued to go to school. Her father owned a school, and he kept it open long after the ban. However, in January of 2009, he had to close it down because of safety issues. So Malala, who loved to learn at her father's school, and everyone else that went there could not learn anymore. Luckily, Malala's father helped her to continue learning. Eventually the government said that girls could go to school, but only for the rest of the school year, to take their exams. They had to wear burqas or else they could not go. Many young girls did not wear them because they did not need to yet. To go back to school though, they had to wear their head coverings. Later, when asked about this, Malala says she feels that girls should wear what they are comfortable in, not what everyone else thinks they should wear.

Eventually, the Taliban figured out who she was. Malala was riding home from school on the bus when some soldiers stopped it. They asked where Malala was, but she did not say anything. They saw her. They shot at her, hitting her, and two of her friends. Her friends were fine, other than being slightly hurt and terrified. However, Malala, who was only 13, was hit with a bullet near her brain, and was knocked unconscious. She was taken to Rawnalpaldi Institute of Cardiology, but they could not help her there. So, she was sent to Queen Elizabeth Hospital in Birmingham. There, they removed part of her skull, because her brain was swelling up. She was in a coma for 10 days after the shooting. Many people were concerned about Malala, such as Barack Obama, Madonna, Hillary Clinton, Angelina Jolie, Laura Bush, and many, many more. Pro-Pakistan-Taliban said that Malala was an American spy (though she was not). They claim that this is why she was shot, though the real reason is she made them mad. She spoke out against them.

Malala Berlin Wall

Once she recovered, she realized that the shooting only made her stronger. In 2011, she won Pakistan's National Peace Prize. Malala was even the first girl to earn the International Children's Peace Prize in 2012.

In 2013, she won the Sakharov Prize. She also co-founded the Malala Fund with Shiza Shadid in 2013. It is in an effort to help all girls get 12 years of a safe, free, and quality education. The Malala Fund has grown into an international (or worldwide) movement. The year 2013 was a good one for Malala, as she also wrote her autobiography, *I am Malala*.

She was not done winning prizes just yet. She shared the 2014 Nobel Peace Prize with Kailash Satyarthi. She was only 17, making her the youngest person to win the Nobel Peace Prize. She is definitely a woman for the history and the record books.

She won all of these prizes because she was not afraid to speak out and change the world. She helped many girls go to school when they would not have been able to go before. She helped people all around the world understand what was happening and how to help fix it.

Malala was the subject of another movie, called *He named me Malala*.

When asked about it, Malala says she has several role models. These include Abdul Ghaffer Khan, Barack Obama, Benazir Bhutto, and most importantly her father. She says that many, many people inspire her, and these are just a few.

Malala at the Oval Office

On 9 November 2021, Malala married Asser Malik in Birmingham. She was able to have that happy conclusion, by marrying her true love.

Malala is an amazing woman who knows the importance of learning. She knew that no matter what, she needed to fight for what was right. Even after she was shot, she continued to fight back. Can you fight for what is right at your school? Has someone hurt your feelings before? If so, how can you tell them what is right in a nice way, just like Malala?

Malala and her Father

I love how kind and loving Malala is, even though everyone was mean, and hateful towards her.

"We need to encourage girls that their voice matters. I think there are hundreds and thousands of Malala's out there."

Visit Malala at her website at: https://malala.org/.

Chapter Four:
Amelia Earhart- The Defier

"Women, like men, should try to do the impossible. And when they fail, their failure should be a challenge to others."

Amelia Mary Earhart was born on July 24, 1897 in Atchison, Kansas. She was half-American, half German. Her sister Muriel and many others called her by the nickname Meeley. Do you have a nickname?

Many people said that Meeley was a tomboy. A tomboy is a girl who acts and dresses more like a boy than a girl. She hated dresses, and wanted to do all the things that only boys were allowed to do. Therefore, she did those things, though she got in trouble a lot for it.

She lived with her grandparents for some time when she was little. She liked it there, but her grandmother was strict, which Amelia did not like.

When she was young, she created a "rollercoaster" that was almost immediately banned by her grandmother. She said it was so fun and exciting, but her grandmother told her that it was not well mannered, so she was not allowed to build another one.

When Meeley was ten, she saw an airplane for the first time. However, she was not impressed by it. She described it as "a thing of rusty wire and wood and not at all interesting".

Amelia was homeschooled until seventh grade. She then went to public school. She learned that she loved to read.

When Meeley was a little bit older, her father came home drunk almost every day. He kept saying that he would stop, but he never did. He eventually lost his job because of this. He said he gave into peer pressure, but he kept drinking repeatedly.

Around this time her grandmother also died. Amelia was very sad about this. The whole family was sad, and was struggling. Amelia said that this was the point when her childhood died.

Ever since Meeley was a little girl, she always knew she wanted to have her own career. Therefore, in 1917, she became a nurse for the Red Cross. There, the 21 year old handed out food and medication, and found an interest in flying. She had the Spanish flu or pneumonia while working for the Red Cross. She probably got it from one of the patients she was helping. She obviously recovered well.

One day, she and her friend decided to do something fun. They went to an airshow. There, an ace, or a pilot that served in a war, dived at the crowd, making everyone run away. However, Amelia stayed exactly where she was. She said that this was when she found out that she wanted to fly. She even got to fly in a plane for 10 minutes for $10. After that, she knew she wanted to be the one flying.

Amelia and Her Twin Engine Plane

Amelia tried many times to be in college, but she hated it. Therefore, instead of going to college, she decided to pay for flight instruction. She got 12 hours of instruction from Neta Snook, which she had to pay off. That meant she had to have a job to pay for it. She ended up having quite a few jobs. She worked as a photographer, truck driver, teacher, social worker and stenographer at the local telephone company to pay for the instruction.

Amelia Earhart with Co Pilot Friend

On October 22, 1922, Amelia flew her plane to an altitude, or height, of 14,000 feet, setting a world record for female pilots. This is just one of the many feats she accomplished. On May 16, 1923, she became the 16th woman in the United States to be issued a pilot's license.

Amelia owned many planes. She gave many of them nicknames such as her "Canary" and her "Yellow Peril". She loved her planes!

Amelia was a writer also. She wrote for a newspaper several times, promoting women flyers.

Because Amelia looked like Charles Linburg, she was nicknamed "Lady Lindy" by the press. She was also known as the "Queen of the Air" She had another nickname, A.E., from her fashion line. She was also part of the Ninety-Nines, a women's flying group.

In 1929, Amelia flew across the Atlantic with Wilmer Stultz. Nevertheless, she did not fly at all! Wilmer did all the flying, and Amelia was not happy that she was not the one flying.

A.E. continued breaking records by being the first woman to fly solo nonstop across the Atlantic. She also was the first *person* to fly from Honolulu to Oakland, California.

For all of Meely's amazing accomplishments, she received many awards, and from many different countries. A few of these were The Distinguished Flying Cross from Congress, the Cross of Knight of the Legion of Honor from the French Government, and the Gold Medal of the National Geographic Society.

Ameilia Earhart and Duke Kahanamoku in Hawaii

Amelia was such a free spirit that George Putman had to ask her to marry him six times! She finally said yes, but under conditions. "I want you to understand I shall not hold you to any medieval code of faithfulness to me nor shall I consider myself bound to you similarly." She continued, "I may have to keep some place where I can go to be by myself, now and then, for I cannot guarantee to endure at all times the confinement of even an attractive cage." She was married to Mr. Putman on February 7, 1931.

Amelia was not finished with her career plans. She was planning a circumnavigational flight. This means that she was going to go all the way around the world, stopping in a few places to get gas. She needed help so she chose Fred Noonan to help her know where she was going.

On her travel around the world, she had lots of engine trouble and sometimes had trouble getting off the ground. Her plane was too heavy with fuel. She even had to start over again. Have you had to start over on something you have tried to do? That is perfectly fine if you have.

Everything was going well until they got close to Howland Island. She contacted the Itasca, a boat that was helping them know where to go, to figure out where she was. They knew she was running out of gas. They could hear her. Unfortunately, she could not hear them.

A log kept by the sailors aboard the Itasca reported that she said,

"WE MUST BE ON YOU BUT CANNOT SEE U BUT GAS IS RUNNING LOW BEEN UNABLE TO REACH YOU BY RADIO WE ARE FLYING AT A 1000 FEET" After that, she was never heard from again.

People all over the world have been searching for any sign of her or her plane since that day. Nothing has ever been found. The mystery remains.

There are many ideas of what happened to her, some more plausible than not. Most people believed that she crashed into the sea and sank. Another theory is that she and Noonan crash landed on a different island, survived, but were never found. Some people have also said the Japanese might have captured her. Another wild theory is that either she was a spy, or she assumed another identity.

Because Amelia Earheart was such an inspirational person, she is still celebrated today. We learn about her from the many, many books about her. Sometimes schools teach about her. People even hold memorial flights in her honor.

Amelia Earhart and Eleanor Roosevelt

What can you do to make a difference in someone's life? It does not have to be big either! How can you help to change the way the world thinks about something you love?

"Never do things others can do and will do if there are things others cannot do or will not do."

Chapter 5:
Princess Diana- The Giver

"Anywhere I see suffering, that is where I want to be, doing what I can."

Diana Frances Spencer was born on July 1, 1961. She is the fourth child out of five. The child born before her died before she was born, so she only had three other siblings. Diana's parents got divorced when she was seven, and she lived with her dad for the most part. Do you know someone whose parents have gotten divorced?

Soon after the divorce, her father was remarried to a woman named Raine. Diana's relationship with her stepmother was not a good one, as she thought of Raine as a bully. One time Diana even pushed her down the stairs. Later, she said that her childhood was "very unstable, the whole thing."

Diana was homeschooled for the first part of her school career by her governess Gertrude Allen. Have you ever been homeschooled?

After that, she was sent to Silfield Private School when she was nine. She was not a schoolchild. In fact, she had to retry her O-levels twice (an O-level is the same as earning a high school diploma).

Diana much preferred to help in the community. She also loved to dance. She was an excellent pianist, swimmer, diver, and ballerina. She even studied tap dance for a while.

Diana was an independent person. She always had a job until she was married. She worked as a nanny, dance instructor, and a playgroup preschool assistant. She loved working with little kids.

Diana as a Kindergarten Teacher

Diana met her future husband on a grouse (a duck like bird) hunting trip. At the time, he was dating her older sister Sarah. The two fell in love after going on 13 dates. He then proposed to her at Windsor Castle, after a short couple of months. They kept their engagement a secret for two and a half weeks after.

The two got married on July 29, 1981. It was known around the world as the Fairy Tale Wedding. In fact, in 2021, a piece of the couple's wedding cake sold for $2,500.

On June 21, 1982, barely a year after their wedding, The Princess of Wales had her first son, Prince William. Two years later, Di had her second son, Harry. He was born on September 15, 1984.

Diana gave her sons more experiences than was usual for princes. She even picked out the schools they went to and the clothes they got to wear, even though most princesses would not be able to do that. Diana said that Harry was "naughty, just like me", and William was "my little wise old man." Which one do you think you are more like?

Diana suffered from an eating disorder called bulimia, which meant she would eat the food, but throw it back up every day. She also struggled with the press. She hated them and would always push them away. One time, she even turned off a camera when she walked up to a man filming her and her sons skiing.

Diana's Wedding Picture

In July of 1996, Charles and Diana agreed on the terms of their divorce and then were separated. Her happily ever after with Prince Charming did not work out. However, she was happier on her own, doing her own things.

Diana loved to work for charities. She went to many, many charity events. In 1991, she helped 397 different charities in just one year. She also enjoyed traveling the world and visiting those who were in need.

Lady Di met many influential people (influential means important or to make an influence on someone). However, more importantly was that she met with, talked to, and took care of not influential people. Most of them had diseases, and many of these diseases were contagious. She made a big impact on the public by hugging a 7-year-old girl with AIDS, which was not something anyone did due to contagiousness. She proved to them that these people deserved love even if they were sick. She helped humanize those with AIDS, HIV, and leprosy.

Once, Diana was walking through a cemetery. She saw a young mother who was crying over the grave of her son. Diana walked over to her and gave her a hug. She said nothing, as they spoke different languages, but that did not stop Diana from trying to comfort someone in need. This is a prime example of who Diana was and what she stood for.

Diana was able to meet Mother Teresa, another very influential woman of her time. They ended up being great friends who met several times over the years.

Diana's Charity Work

In 1987, Diana was awarded the Freedom of the City of London which is the highest honor bestowed by the city of London. She was a great choice, because she was an amazing person that was able to help change the world so that it was better for everyone.

The people loved Diana. She was nicknamed "The People's Princess" because they loved her and she loved them. The obsession over her was named "Dianamania." Unfortunately, the people's obsession with Diana became a problem, as well as ultimately the cause of her death. The press started to make it so that Diana had NO privacy, even when she was on vacation. Wouldn't you get annoyed with them too?

Diana, Charles, Nancy Reagan and President Ronald Reagan

Princess Di was killed in a car crash in Paris on August 31, 1997. The paparazzi (or a photographer who takes pictures of celebrities, usually without their permission) were chasing her. The driver was trying to get her away from them. He was going extremely fast. This resulted in her death. Dodi Fayed, her companion, and the driver, Henri Paul, were also killed.

32.10 million people watched the televised funeral. So many people loved her, and they were all sad to see her go.

There are many tributes to the princess, such as postage stamps, wax statues, tributes, and many other memorial sites all over the world. She was such an amazing person that she is celebrated all around the world. She is known by many people and is still talked about a lot today.

Diana loved everyone no matter what. She gave all that she could to people that not very many people cared about. She made sure everyone felt loved, even when there were big differences between the two people. She was not afraid of caring for those with disease. How can you show love to other people? How can you help the people that no one else likes?

"I don't go by the rule book... I lead from the heart, not the head."

Epilogue

Dear Reader,

Don't you think those girls are just amazing? I agree. They make me want to be a better person. They make me want to find something I can do to change the world in my own special way.

That is what I want you to do. I want you to find a way that you can make your world a better place. How can you be special?

I told you of some ways to be like these girls, but what if the things that these girls did are not the things you are good at, things you don't like to do, then find something you like to do. Most of these girls were just doing what they loved, and it ended up being that they helped change the world because of it. I want every girl to find something that is her thing. Maybe your thing is being an inspirational Youtuber that helps people love themselves. Maybe you are meant to be a teacher to help kids learn and grow. Who knows, maybe you will even be the first woman president (if so, that is super cool)! I say shoot for the stars and never let anyone knock you down. You got this!

I want you to know you are loved. Even if you do not think you are, someone in this world loves you so much.

One of my favorite quotes is

"To the world, you may be one person, but to one person, you may be the world." Dr. Seuss.

This world is big, but we can make it better one person at a time. One house at a time. One neighborhood at a time. You can make a difference no matter who you are.

One of the things that I want to stress is that men and women are equal. So are blacks and whites. Gay or straight. Religious or not. We are all the same. We are all good enough. *You* are good enough. Do not let any person tell you that you are not strong enough, pretty enough, anything enough. Because you are. You are great because you are you. So never, *ever* let anyone change you. Do not be someone for someone else. Be you *for* you.

Lastly, I want to say that you deserve to have all of the things that we can't/couldn't do. You are worthy, you are deserving.

You are AMAZING!

Love,
Isabelle Thrapp

www.ingramcontent.com/pod-product-compliance
Lightning Source LLC
LaVergne TN
LVHW061049070526
838201LV00074B/5227